Original title:
Spinning Solitude

Copyright © 2024 Creative Arts Management OÜ
All rights reserved.

Author: Mariana Leclair
ISBN HARDBACK: 978-9916-90-734-4
ISBN PAPERBACK: 978-9916-90-735-1

The Morning After Quiet

The dawn creeps in so slow,
Whispers of night let go.
Soft light breaks through the trees,
As peace dances on the breeze.

Birds sing a tender song,
The world is waking strong.
Dewdrops shimmer on the grass,
Moments of stillness, they amass.

A cup of warmth in hand,
Life begins to understand.
Each shadow fades away,
In the promise of the day.

The morning after quiet,
Leaves room for heart's riot.
With the sun's gentle touch,
Hope rises, bright and much.

Vortex of Thoughts

Spiraling in a wild dash,
Ideas clash, a potent thrash.
Whispers echo in my mind,
A labyrinth, so hard to find.

Words float like autumn leaves,
Dancing softly, then it leaves.
Caught in the swirling air,
Each notion, a silent prayer.

In this tempest, I must steer,
Through the chaos, I hold dear.
Moments flash, then slip away,
In the vortex of the day.

Yet in the storm, there's a calm,
A flicker of a healing balm.
Thoughts may race, but I will find,
The peace within, the quiet kind.

Twilight of the Hidden

Shadows stretch across the land,
Mysteries hidden, softly stand.
The horizon blushes red,
In this dusk, where dreams are fed.

Whispers weave through twilight air,
Secrets linger, everywhere.
Stars begin to light the night,
Guiding ghosts with gentle light.

Beneath the cloak of darkened skies,
Hidden truths, like fireflies.
Each glimmer tells a tale untold,
In the evening's grip, behold.

As day succumbs to night's decree,
In silence, the world breathes free.
Twilight holds the keys to see,
The beauty in what's yet to be.

Shadows of an Abandoned Heart

In the quiet dusk, shadows creep,
Memories linger, secrets they keep.
Whispers of love, now faded and dark,
A vacant echo in the hollowed park.

Ghosts of laughter, lost in the wind,
A tale of sorrow, where hope has thinned.
Once vibrant dreams, now muted and grey,
In the stillness of night, they silently sway.

Solace in the Silent Hours

Under the moon, in cloaked embrace,
Time stands still, a gentle grace.
Stars above, like thoughts, they gleam,
In the quiet, we find our dream.

Moments stretched like stretches of silk,
Whispers of night, sweet as milk.
In the calm, our fears dissolve,
A soft resolve, the heart's sweet solve.

Whirlwinds of the Unseen Self

Inside the mind, the chaos swirls,
Fragments dance, like fleeting pearls.
A tempest brewing, hidden so deep,
Within the silence, the secrets we keep.

Flickers of doubt, like shadows they play,
Lost in the maze, we fade away.
Yet in the storm, courage may rise,
To face the truth that never lies.

Fragmented Thoughts in Twilight

As day concedes to the night's soft glow,
Thoughts like fireflies begin to flow.
Each flicker bright, then lost in the dark,
A tapestry woven with hope's small spark.

Unraveled dreams lie scattered wide,
In twilight's embrace, they painfully bide.
Yet with each breath, we seek to reclaim,
The scattered pieces, the lost in the flame.

A Breath of Distance

On the edge of twilight's glow,
Whispers linger soft and slow.
Across valleys, shadows play,
Time drifts silently away.

Footsteps fade upon the sand,
Waves retreat at nature's hand.
In the air, a longing sigh,
Dreams unfold, as night draws nigh.

Stars awaken, twinkling bright,
Guiding souls through velvet night.
Each heart beats at its own pace,
Finding solace in this space.

Distance breathes a gentle tune,
Underneath the silver moon.
With every sigh, a story told,
In echoes soft, memories hold.

The Still Waters Run Deep

Mirror calm reflecting grace,
Beneath the surface, shadows trace.
Where secrets dwell, old whispers weep,
In the silence, still waters keep.

Time flows gentle, like a stream,
Life unfolds like a tender dream.
Ripples dance on the quiet face,
In the depths, hidden truths embrace.

Moonlight dances, casting gold,
On still waters, stories told.
Dreamers pause, hearts set free,
In this moment, they can be.

Echoes call from leaves above,
Nature's hymn, a song of love.
In stillness lies a world unbound,
Where peace and hope are always found.

The Echo Chamber

Voices bounce within these walls,
Softly rising, tender calls.
In the chamber, hearts align,
Echoes weave, their threads entwine.

Words repeat from ear to ear,
Carried forth by hope and fear.
Resonating through the night,
Lost in echoes, seeking light.

In this space, thoughts take flight,
Carried on the wings of night.
Silent prayers, whispers blend,
In the echoes, souls transcend.

Stillness cradles fleeting dreams,
As the world is torn at seams.
Yet in the chamber, love remains,
A refuge found in heart's refrain.

The Silent Waltz

Amidst the shadows, silence glides,
Where gentle movements softly bide.
Two souls sway in the quiet air,
A waltz unspoken, a tender prayer.

Footsteps light on dusted floor,
In the stillness, they explore.
Every glance, a story spun,
Two hearts dancing, becoming one.

Whispers linger in the night,
As moonbeams cast a silver light.
In this dance, the world stands still,
In every moment, time does thrill.

When music fades, and shadows blend,
Lost in a rhythm, they transcend.
In silent waltz, forever free,
Together they write their symphony.

A World of One

In shadows deep where I reside,
A single heart, a mind to hide.
The silence speaks, a constant hum,
In this small space, I come undone.

A fragile world within my grasp,
No hands to hold, no friend to clasp.
Yet in the stillness, thoughts entwine,
A universe that feels divine.

With every breath, I carve my way,
Through whispered dreams that softly play.
It's here I find my rarest grace,
In solitude, I find my place.

Yet time drips slow like melting snow,
And in this realm, the shadows grow.
A world of one, both vast and small,
I stand alone but hear it call.

Frayed Edges of Contemplation

Thoughts unravel like frayed thread,
In quiet nooks where shadows spread.
I trace the lines of what has been,
In whispered tones, I search within.

Each moment folds like ancient lore,
Time spills its secrets on the floor.
The edges blur, the boundaries blend,
Where does the journey start or end?

With every flicker of the mind,
New paths emerge, new truths to find.
In silent questions that await,
I dig for meaning, contemplate.

The frayed edges call, beckoning me,
To step into the mystery.
With every thought, a thread is spun,
In contemplation, I am one.

Distant Echoes of Self

In the halls of memory I roam,
Echoes of laughter, a distant home.
Reflections dance in twilight's glow,
Fragments of who I used to know.

Faded faces flicker like dreams,
In haunting whispers, the heart redeems.
I chase the shadows, I seek the light,
In every echo, a glimpse of flight.

Through corridors of long-lost time,
I grapple with rhythm, I learn to climb.
Each step reveals a deeper tale,
The echoes guide where words might fail.

In distant sounds, I hear my voice,
In solitude, I make my choice.
To embrace the past, and all it holds,
In distant echoes, my heart unfolds.

The Pulse of Isolation

In the stillness, a heartbeat sounds,
A thrum of life in empty grounds.
Loneliness wraps its gentle shawl,
In quiet corners, I hear it call.

The pulse of thoughts, a steady beat,
In solitude, I find retreat.
The world outside feels far away,
Yet in this silence, I learn to stay.

I hear my doubts, I gather dreams,
In the solitude, a light gleams.
With every breath, I deepen roots,
Isolation brings its hidden fruits.

Though shadows linger, I stand tall,
In the pulse of isolation, I answer the call.
With open arms, I embrace the night,
For in this solitude, I find my light.

A Journey Within

In shadows deep, I tread alone,
Where whispers echo, thoughts have flown.
Each step a question, who am I?
In silence vast, the answers lie.

A winding path through doubt and grace,
Reflections dance, I see my face.
With every heartbeat, fears unwind,
The light within is what I find.

Through valleys low and peaks so high,
I gather strength; I learn to fly.
In the stillness, truth does bloom,
A journey made within the womb.

So here I stand, my soul laid bare,
With every breath, I shed despair.
The journey's long, yet here I stay,
Inward bound, I find my way.

The Lament of Lonesomeness

A solitary tear does fall,
In the silence, echoes call.
Empty chairs and vacant rooms,
Whispering of unfilled blooms.

The clock ticks on, a haunting sound,
Each minute lost, forever found.
In shadows where the memories lie,
I search the night, but only sigh.

Stars above seem far away,
In the stillness, dreams decay.
Hope flickers dim, a distant star,
Yet in my heart, it's never far.

So here I stand, in twilight's glow,
With every sigh, the feelings grow.
The lament plays a tender tune,
Of lonesomeness beneath the moon.

Solitary Serenade

In twilight's hush, the world does fade,
A gentle song, my heart has made.
Each note a wish, so soft and light,
In solitude, I find my flight.

The wind it sings a lonesome tune,
Underneath the silver moon.
With every breath, I tune my heart,
In this dance, I learn my part.

A melody of whispered dreams,
In quiet moments, hope redeems.
With strings of silence, I compose,
A serenade that softly glows.

So let me drift in this embrace,
With solitude, I find my grace.
In every note, a piece is free,
This solitary symphony.

Cradle of Quietude

In the hush of night, a cradle sways,
Where dreams are born in tender ways.
Beneath the stars, the world does rest,
In quietude, I feel so blessed.

The whispers of the wind so slight,
Wrap me close in soft twilight.
Each breath a lullaby divine,
In every pause, the heart will shine.

I find my peace in shadows deep,
Where thoughts can wander, freely leap.
In this embrace, I close my eyes,
And drift away to starlit skies.

So here I dwell, in stillness true,
A cradle holds my spirit too.
In quietude, the soul will mend,
A gentle journey with no end.

A Choreography of Unheard Voices

In shadows deep, they sway and spin,
Voices lost, where dreams begin.
A dance of thoughts, so soft and shy,
Whispers flutter, as moments fly.

Each step a tale, through time it flows,
In silent grace, the spirit knows.
Guided by heartbeats, they take their chance,
A choreography of an unseen dance.

Echoes linger, in every sigh,
A symphony of why and why.
In stillness found, they weave and part,
Unheard voices, an artful heart.

Bound by silence, yet never alone,
In this space, their truth is sown.
Together they rise, like morning's dew,
A beautiful chaos, forever new.

The Quiet Symphony of One

In solitude, a melody plays,
A whispering tune that softly sways.
Notes of silence fill the air,
An echo of thoughts, light as a prayer.

Each breath a beat, a timely reprieve,
A symphony crafted, we dare to believe.
Harmony blooms in the still of the night,
One voice awakens, igniting the light.

Strings of loneliness, gently entwined,
Compose a ballad, pure and refined.
In quiet moments, we find our space,
A singular soul, in a vast embrace.

The heart conducts, with tender hands,
A score of existence, it quietly stands.
In the vastness of one, all can find,
The quiet symphony, within the mind.

Silent Threads of Time's Weaving

In the loom of days, threads intertwine,
Woven discreetly, like whispers divine.
Patterns of moments, both fragile and bold,
Silent stories in colors untold.

Time moves gently, a needle in flight,
Sewing the fabric of day into night.
Each stitch a heartbeat, each knot a sigh,
In the tapestry's embrace, we learn to fly.

Echoes of laughter, shadows of tears,
Every thread carries hopes and fears.
Woven with care, in harmony's bind,
Silent threads, by fate designed.

At the edge of the fabric, futures await,
A delicate weave, we call our fate.
In stillness we find, life's sweetest chime,
Silent threads, in the rivers of time.

In the Company of Shadows

In dim-lit corners, where shadows blend,
A dance of silence, we comprehend.
Figures embrace, in flickering light,
The company of shadows feels just right.

They gather close, in whispers profound,
Secrets shared without a sound.
In twilight's glow, they come alive,
In the hush of dusk, the spirits thrive.

With every heartbeat, they sway and recoil,
Bound in the moment, their essence uncoil.
A tapestry woven of dreams and despair,
In the company of shadows, laid bare.

Together they linger, in stories untold,
Tracing the edges of the brave and the bold.
In the shadows we find, not fear but grace,
In their quiet presence, we all find a place.

Lullabies for the Lonely Soul

In the hush of night, shadows creep,
Gentle murmurs, the secrets they keep,
Stars above sing, softly they glow,
Cradling dreams in a tender flow.

Whispers of hope in the quiet air,
Flickers of warmth in the cool despair,
Close your eyes, let the silence embrace,
Find your solace in this sacred space.

Moonlight dances on the silent sea,
Easing sorrows, setting hearts free,
Waves of comfort, a soft serenade,
Lull the lonely, in twilight's shade.

With each breath, let the worries fade,
In the stillness, dreams are made,
Lullabies wrap you in gentle light,
Guide your spirit through the night.

Reveries of a Wandering Mind

In fields of thought, the wildflowers sway,
Lost in the dreams that drift and play,
Clouds like whispers float overhead,
Painting visions where silence is bred.

Paths untraveled, a dance of the free,
Mapping the world in my reverie,
Each thought a star in the boundless sky,
Wings of imagination, ready to fly.

Moments linger in the softest hues,
Echoes of laughter, the sweetest news,
Time slips by as I wander afar,
Guided by the light of my inner star.

In the tapestry of dreams I weave,
Fleeting glimpses of what I believe,
A mosaic of hopes, so bright and bold,
In the heart of a mind that longs to unfold.

The Still Waters of a Thinker's Stream

In tranquil pools where thoughts reside,
Ripples form, like a gentle tide,
Reflections dance on the surface clear,
Each moment whispers what we hold dear.

Beneath the calm, the currents flow,
Secrets swirling, yet soft and slow,
With every thought, a world is born,
In the quiet depths, the mind is worn.

Seeping wisdom from roots below,
Branches stretch where the wild winds blow,
In the stillness, clarity finds a way,
To guide the lost through the dusk of day.

As dusk descends, the waters gleam,
Nurtured by the night's soft dream,
Each question lingers, a star above,
In the still waters, we learn to love.

Whispered Wishes in the Abyss

In caverns deep, where shadows sigh,
Wishes echo, a silent cry,
From the depths, a hope takes flight,
Guided by whispers in the night.

The abyss holds stories of hearts unseen,
Each wish a shimmer, a fragile sheen,
Casting lines into the void so wide,
Search for solace, let dreams abide.

With every heartbeat, a longing grows,
In the silence, deep yearning flows,
To the edge of time, I send my plea,
In the darkness, I learn to be free.

Whispered secrets of the soul's despair,
In that silence, I find my prayer,
Wishing upon the stars up high,
In the abyss, my hopes will fly.

Ocean of Solitary Thoughts

Waves crash softly on the shore,
Carrying dreams from days of yore.
Reflections dance on silvery tides,
Where my hidden heart confides.

Endless blue, a vast expanse,
In solitude, I find my trance.
Each ripple holds a whispered thought,
In this ocean, solace sought.

A ship adrift, with sails unfurled,
Navigating through a quiet world.
Voices lost in the salty air,
In my heart, they linger there.

Beneath the stars, the night unfolds,
Secrets of the deep it holds.
In every wave, I find my peace,
In this ocean, my thoughts release.

Starlit Paths Through Solitude's Veil

Beneath a sky of glimmering light,
I wander alone through the night.
Paths of silver, softly glowed,
In solitude, my heart have sowed.

Echoes whisper through the trees,
Carrying secrets on the breeze.
Footsteps light on the cool, damp ground,
In this silence, solace found.

As constellations guide my way,
The shadows dance, begin to sway.
Each star a witness to my plight,
Illuminating my inner fight.

Through valleys deep and hills so high,
In solitude, I learn to fly.
With every breath, I reclaim my fate,
On starlit paths, I contemplate.

Whispers in the Quiet

In the stillness, shadows creep,
Where thoughts awaken from their sleep.
Whispers echo in the air,
Filling spaces, standing bare.

A single leaf falls to the ground,
In the silence, a soft sound.
Nature holds her breath for me,
In this calm, my soul is free.

Hidden truths begin to speak,
Secrets linger, soft and meek.
In quiet moments, wisdom thrives,
Where the heart and spirit strives.

Through gentle winds, the silence thrills,
Carrying echoes of distant hills.
In the hush, the world feels near,
In whispers soft, I find my cheer.

Threads of Isolation

Stitching moments with quiet thread,
In my mind, a tapestry spread.
Each fiber holds a memory dear,
In isolation, I persevere.

The loom of life weaves stories tight,
Shadows weaving with the light.
Fingers tracing paths of sorrow,
In each stitch, I find tomorrow.

A solitary dance of fate,
In the silence, I meditate.
Each thread a journey woven with care,
In isolation, a love laid bare.

Through the fabric, hope entwines,
In the stillness, life aligns.
These threads connect my heart to dreams,
In this solitude, freedom gleams.

Footprints in the Sand

Upon the shore where silence reigns,
Two footprints mark the soft terrain.
The tide rolls in, a gentle sweep,
To erase the memories we keep.

With every wave, our paths are lost,
Yet love remains, no matter the cost.
The sun will set, the night will spread,
But in our hearts, the light is fed.

Whispers in the wind softly call,
Reminding us of one and all.
As footprints fade, we stand anew,
In the dance of waves, our love shines through.

A Canvas of Emptiness

In the quiet void where shadows play,
A canvas waits for hues of gray.
Each stroke a breath, a fleeting thought,
In the silence, battles fought.

A brush of hope, a splash of fear,
Creating worlds we hold so dear.
Yet emptiness, a ghostly friend,
In its depths, we seek to mend.

The colors blend, they come alive,
From nothingness, we learn to thrive.
On this canvas, we write our tale,
In shades of joy, and shades of pale.

The Solitary Spiral

In solitude, a spiral twines,
A journey etched in hidden signs.
Each curve a thought, each line a tear,
Winding paths that draw us near.

Through darkest times, the spiral grows,
In quiet strength, our spirit knows.
With every turn, a lesson learned,
In stillness found, the heart has burned.

As echoes fade, we find our way,
In the solitude, we learn to stay.
A spiral dance, a sacred truth,
In cycles deep, lies the heart of youth.

The Hidden Harmony

Amidst the noise, a song is sung,
In whispered notes, the world is strung.
The hidden chords of life entwine,
A symphony, divine, benign.

Through tangled thoughts, the rhythm flows,
In quiet spaces, beauty grows.
Each heartbeat echoes in the night,
A harmony beyond our sight.

And in the silence, secrets bloom,
Life's sweetest sounds dispel the gloom.
In hidden tones, we find our place,
In harmony, we embrace grace.

Portrait of a Quiet Heart

In the stillness, whispers dwell,
Soft echoes of a secret spell.
A canvas painted with serene grace,
Each stroke tells of a hidden place.

Gentle breaths of twilight air,
Caress the thoughts, light as a prayer.
In shadows deep, calm feelings bloom,
A quiet heart finds peace in gloom.

Moments linger, time stands still,
A tranquil dance amid the chill.
Reflections spark in every sigh,
The silent language of goodbye.

Embrace the quiet, let it reign,
Within the heart, a sweet refrain.
In solitude, a beauty bright,
A portrait framed in soft moonlight.

The Solitude Ballet

In an empty room, silence sways,
The echoes of forgotten days.
A dancer twirls without a sound,
In solitude, her grace is found.

Each movement holds a quiet tale,
Of whispered dreams that softly sail.
She pirouettes on shadow's edge,
In solitude, she makes her pledge.

The mirrors glow with ghostly light,
Reflecting worlds both dark and bright.
Her body weaves through space and time,
In every step, a quiet rhyme.

The stage is bare, yet hearts believe,
In solitude, we learn to grieve.
But in the loss, a beauty grows,
A ballet where the spirit flows.

Whirlwind of Inner Thoughts

Thoughts collide like stormy skies,
A whirlwind spins, the mind complies.
Ideas dance in chaotic flight,
Wrestling dawn, embracing night.

Images flash, a fleeting spark,
In the tempest, there's both light and dark.
Voices whisper, futures call,
Lost in echoes, I rise and fall.

Fragments dart like fireflies,
Through the labyrinth where reason lies.
A cacophony of dreams and fears,
The inner storm, it perseveres.

Yet amid the chaos, clarity glows,
A quiet truth that gently flows.
In the whirlwind, wisdom finds,
The serenity that frees our minds.

Sanctuary of One

In a corner, soft and warm,
A sanctuary protected from harm.
Here the soul can rest its wings,
And listen to the peace it brings.

Walls of silence wrap around,
Here, tranquility is found.
A gentle light, the heart unfolds,
In solitude, the spirit bolds.

Time drips slowly, like sweet rain,
Each moment free from worldly pain.
In this haven, worries cease,
A refuge built on quiet peace.

So guard this place, both still and bright,
Let it cradle you through the night.
In the sanctuary of one, we find,
The deepest essence of the mind.

The Dance of One

In twilight's glow, a figure sways,
Moving softly, lost in a trance,
Shadows stretch, and music plays,
A gentle heart in a quiet dance.

Beneath the stars, the world feels light,
Each step whispers tales of old,
With lingering dreams, they take flight,
Embracing a rhythm, bold yet controlled.

Steps entwined, like branches high,
In harmony, they twirl and spin,
Under the vast and endless sky,
A secret language found within.

As night drifts on, the dance won't cease,
In every twirl, a fleeting glance,
Within this world, they find their peace,
Two souls united in the dance.

Embrace of the Echo

Among the hills, the whispers tease,
Echoes bounce on valleys wide,
A symphony played by the breeze,
Nature's song in ebb and tide.

Each voice a thread, a moment's grace,
Carried forth on silken air,
In shadows deep, they find their place,
A gentle chorus, rich and rare.

As twilight fades, the echoes blend,
A dance of voices, soft and near,
In unity, the messages send,
In silence lost, their hearts adhere.

Embracing tones of dusk's embrace,
Their harmony a lasting art,
In every note, a well-loved trace,
An echo shared, a beating heart.

Reflections in Stillness

In mirrored depths, the stillness lies,
A tranquil pond, a glassy dome,
Where thoughts can drift like whispered sighs,
And find a way to call it home.

Leaves above dance with the breeze,
Their shadows flicker on the skin,
In every hush, a moment's ease,
The world around draws deep within.

A fleeting glance of evening's hue,
Broken by ripples soft and slight,
In this calm, where silence grew,
The heart finds all it seeks in night.

Each thought a petal, gently cast,
Upon the water's silent grace,
In stillness, moments hold steadfast,
Reflecting dreams we dare to face.

Woven in Silence

In quiet threads, the tapestry spins,
Softly woven, each moment's hue,
Between the lines where silence grins,
A world created anew.

Colors blend in gentle seams,
The fabric holds a story tight,
In every stitch, a blend of dreams,
Crafted carefully, day and night.

Time unravels in soft embrace,
In whispers lost, a tender bond,
Life's forgetting in a sacred space,
Where hearts are free and love responds.

Woven in silence, a tale unfolds,
Every detail a quiet delight,
In hidden corners, the magic molds,
A masterpiece born of soft twilight.

In Hushed Spaces

Whispers linger in the air,
Soft shadows dance, unaware.
Gentle echoes, quietly found,
In these corners, peace is sound.

Silent moments weave through time,
Rhythms pulse, a tranquil rhyme.
Here, the world begins to fade,
In hushed spaces, fears can trade.

Thoughts float softly, like a sigh,
Underneath the endless sky.
Waves of calm in gentle streams,
In such stillness, hope redeems.

Unseen bonds with every breath,
In the quiet, finds its depth.
In these chambers, hearts can hear,
In hushed spaces, love is near.

The Stillness Speaks

In the pause where shadows blend,
Time's sharp edge begins to bend.
Silence carves the space around,
In this stillness, truth is found.

Glimmers fade, then brightly glow,
In the hush, we come to know.
Words unspoken fill the void,
In this quiet, hearts are buoyed.

Moments linger, softly sway,
Carried on the breath of day.
Listen close, let worries cease,
In the stillness, find your peace.

Every heartbeat tells a tale,
In this calm, the spirits sail.
Faceless shadows dance with grace,
In the stillness, we embrace.

Threads of the Forgotten

Worn memories in faded light,
Whispers tell of day and night.
Once vibrant colors now turned grey,
Threads of old no longer sway.

Frayed edges of a bygone dream,
Quiet echoes, soft and dim.
Stories linger in the air,
Threads of the lost everywhere.

In the corners, dust collects,
Fragile words that time neglects.
Yet in silence, life does cling,
Threads of the past still softly sing.

Each forgotten name holds weight,
Threads that bind us, twist with fate.
In the shadow of the old,
Stories rise, though seldom told.

The Atlas of Alone

Maps of moments left behind,
In the silence, solace find.
Navigating through the night,
In the shadows, seek the light.

Landscapes stretch with heart and bone,
Every journey leads alone.
Yet in solitude, we grow,
In this atlas, paths will flow.

Stars above, a guiding spark,
Illumination in the dark.
Every step a tale to tell,
In each heartbeat, find the swell.

Bridges built from whispered dreams,
Across rivers, love redeems.
Even when we walk apart,
In this atlas, beats one heart.

Moments of Introspection

In the mirror, I see my soul,
Layers of dreams, both fractured and whole.
Thoughts drift softly, like autumn leaves,
Whispers of hopes that time never cleaves.

Each breath reveals what's left unsaid,
In quiet corners, my heart has bled.
A tapestry woven with threads of fear,
A journey of shadows that draws me near.

The clock ticks slowly, seconds stretch wide,
In stillness, the secrets of life abide.
Moments of doubt dance in the light,
Yet courage ignites within the night.

Here in silence, I claim my space,
Embracing the scars that time can't erase.
In every reflection, I find a key,
Unlocking the depths that are buried in me.

Diary of a Whisper

In the hush of night, secrets unfold,
Stories of hearts in whispers retold.
Pages turn softly, ink kissed by fate,
Unraveling dreams before it's too late.

The echoes of laughter, the sighs, the screams,
Captured in shadows, alive in my dreams.
Each word a footprint, lost in the sand,
A diary written by fate's gentle hand.

Moments of silence hold treasures untold,
The warmth of a glance, a love story bold.
In the dance of the leaves, I hear your name,
A whisper resurfaces, forever the same.

Each tear that falls writes a new line,
A melody soft, both tender and fine.
In stillness, the heart learns to sing,
Embracing the joy that tomorrow may bring.

The Quiet Tides

Waves crash softly on the silent shore,
Rhythms echo, revealing much more.
Under the moonlight, secrets reside,
In the stillness, the world feels wide.

Footprints trail off, lost in the sand,
Whispers of nature, gentle and grand.
The tide pulls back, revealing shells bright,
Stories of ages bathed in moonlight.

Gulls cry above in the crisp, cool air,
Bringing old tales, forgotten with care.
Each ebb and flow, a lesson bestowed,
In the heart of the ocean, wisdom is sowed.

As dawn approaches, the colors ignite,
Painting the sky in soft hues of light.
In the quiet moments, peace will abide,
Forever remembered in the quiet tides.

Cornered by Stillness

In the corner of time where silence dwells,
Echoes of thought, like distant bells.
Walls of my mind, both close and opaque,
A fortress of dreams that time cannot break.

Shadows weave gently through moments laid bare,
A dance of reflection, a breath of despair.
In solitude's arms, I find my refrain,
A symphony echoing joy mixed with pain.

Cornered by stillness, each heartbeat I feel,
An orchestra plays, revealing what's real.
With every regret, there's growth in disguise,
In moments of quiet, wisdom arises.

So here I will sit, embraced by the calm,
Centering self with each tender balm.
In silence, I bloom, like a flower in spring,
Finding my voice in the stillness I bring.

Beneath Layers of Silence

Whispers hide in muted tones,
The heartbeats echo in quiet zones.
A veil of calm, a soothing frost,
In stillness found, we seldom lost.

A thousand thoughts drift like the breeze,
Settling gently in the trees.
Moments linger, soft and pure,
In silence reigns, the soul's allure.

Each breath a note in nature's song,
Carried forth, where dreams belong.
Beneath the layers, truth awaits,
In tranquil depths, love resonates.

With every sigh, a world unfolds,
Stories untold and yet so bold.
Dive deep within, embrace the peace,
In silence found, our thoughts release.

In the Wake of Shadows

Night drapes softly on the ground,
In shadows deep, lost souls are found.
Faint echoes of a life once bright,
Fade into the depths of night.

Footsteps linger on the stone,
Whispers beckon, we're not alone.
The moonlight dances, a fleeting glance,
In the dark, we dare to take a chance.

As dawn approaches, dreams take flight,
Chasing away remnants of night.
In the wake of shadows past,
We find the strength to hold on fast.

Hope arises with the sun's first beam,
Shattering the night, igniting the dream.
And though the shadows may persist,
In their depths, we find our bliss.

Horizons of Reflection

Waves lap gently at sandy shores,
Each ripple hints of distant doors.
Horizon stretched like a painter's dream,
Where thoughts converge and silence gleams.

Mirrored skies in tranquil seas,
Thoughts drift softly with the breeze.
In the depths of azure blue,
Time stands still with a perfect view.

The sun dips low, a golden hue,
Painting visions both old and new.
In this silence, souls align,
Horizons glimmer, hearts entwine.

In reflections, we seek our cheer,
To find the voices that we hold dear.
Beneath the surface, wisdom waits,
In all we are, our fate creates.

The Solitary Capsule

Within the walls of quiet space,
A journey holds a gentle grace.
A capsule formed from dream and thought,
In solitude, the battles fought.

Time ticks slowly, each second sways,
Moments blend, lost in the haze.
A fragile shell that keeps me safe,
In the depths of an inward waif.

Voices whisper in the mist,
Memories linger, too sweet to resist.
In the capsule, dreams ignite,
A beacon shining through the night.

With every pulse, new worlds explore,
Opening doors, seeking more.
In solitude, I find my way,
The solitary heart leads the fray.

Enigmas of the Alone

Whispers dance in the hollow night,
Shadows weave tales without light.
In silence, secrets find their grace,
Each heartbeat echoes, a soft embrace.

Voices linger, yet none to hear,
In solitude's fold, thoughts persevere.
The mind wanders through unseen doors,
Searching for solace on barren shores.

A mirror reflects the depths we hide,
In vacant spaces, thoughts collide.
The enigma of being, a fragile thread,
Tying the living to whispers of dread.

Yet through the shadows, stars emerge,
Illuminating paths where dreams surge.
In the realm of the alone, we grow,
Finding strength in the silent flow.

A Tapestry of Quiet Moments

Threads of silence gently spun,
Capture the warmth of the setting sun.
Each moment woven with care and grace,
In the tapestry, memories find their place.

Soft footsteps on a quiet street,
Where laughter echoes, hearts greet.
A shared glance, a fleeting smile,
In the stillness, time has a style.

The rustle of leaves, a tender sigh,
Nature's chorus, a lullaby.
Every heartbeat in sync with the day,
Crafting the scenes that softly sway.

As dusk descends in shades of blue,
The stars emerge, a tranquil view.
In every quiet moment we find,
A tapestry rich, lovingly entwined.

Musings in Moonlight

Under the glow of silver light,
Thoughts take flight into the night.
The moon whispers secrets to the sea,
In its embrace, we long to be.

Reflected dreams on a tranquil tide,
Waves carry wishes, hearts open wide.
A gentle breeze, a lover's caress,
In moonlit musing, we find our rest.

Stars flicker like hopes in the dark,
Each one a promise, a lingering spark.
In the stillness, we come alive,
Swaying with the night as we thrive.

From shadows emerge the stories untold,
In moonlight's embrace, we break the mold.
Here in the stillness, our spirits soar,
Finding the magic forevermore.

Melodies of the Unseen

In the quiet spaces, music flows,
Harmonies whispered where no one goes.
Each note a ripple in the still air,
A dance of emotions, tender and rare.

The rustle of grass sings a tune,
While shadows flutter beneath the moon.
Every heartbeat creates a refrain,
In the melody, joy and pain.

We hear the silence in its own way,
Notes intertwine, come what may.
A symphony crafted by unseen hands,
Binding our spirits in distant lands.

With every breath, a story unfolds,
In the melody of the brave and the bold.
In unseen realms where dreams convene,
We find our place in the ever-greens.

A Tangle of Thoughts

Whispers of doubt twist and bend,
Racing through corridors, mind won't mend.
A knot of wishes, dreams intertwined,
Searching for solace, a peace to find.

A tapestry woven with threads of fear,
Hopes lost in shadows, the end drawing near.
Yet in this chaos, a spark ignites,
A flicker of courage, illuminating nights.

Each thought a petal, falling from grace,
In the garden of memories, a familiar place.
Collecting the fragments, I learn to embrace,
The beauty in chaos, the art of the chase.

Through the tangle, I wander and roam,
Discovering pathways that lead me home.
In the silence, my heart starts to sing,
A melody rising, my spirit taking wing.

The Art of Alone

In the stillness of the twilight hour,
I find my strength, a quiet power.
Embracing solitude, I learn to grow,
In shadows cast by the moon's soft glow.

With each breath taken, a rhythm found,
In the echoes of silence, my heart's profound.
No voices to drown out the thoughts within,
A canvas of peace where I can begin.

The world fades away, a distant hum,
In the symphony of solitude, I succumb.
Colors bloom in a life all my own,
In the art of alone, my spirit has grown.

Every moment cherished, a chance to reflect,
To understand self, and learn to connect.
In tranquil whispers, I find my place,
The beauty of solitude, a warm embrace.

Chasing Ghosts of Company

In echoes of laughter, shadows creep,
Whispers of memories, secrets to keep.
Chasing the phantoms of friends long gone,
In the stillness, their spirits linger on.

Familiar faces in the corners of thought,
Moments of joy, the battles they fought.
Yet here I stand, a solitary soul,
Searching for closure, to feel whole.

Footsteps trace patterns on paths of despair,
Longing for company, the warmth of a care.
But silence wraps tightly, a comforting shroud,
In the void of the night, I speak to the crowd.

With every ghost held in delicate grace,
A dance of the heart in this empty space.
In chasing their laughter, I learn to belong,
To find peace in the echoes, to continue the song.

Nocturnal Reverie

Under the blanket of star-studded skies,
Dreams take flight with each whispered sighs.
Moonbeams pirouette on the edge of night,
As shadows embrace, surrendering light.

Thoughts weave like constellations above,
In this tranquil space, I feel the love.
The world asleep, yet my spirit ignites,
In the dance of the darkness, the heart takes flight.

A realm of wonder where time stands still,
Whispers of wishes on the soft night chill.
Holding the stillness, I breathe in deep,
In nocturnal reverie, my soul finds sleep.

The dreams become vivid, a tapestry spun,
In the quietest hours, new journeys begun.
As dawn breaks gently, the beauty remains,
In the magic of night, my spirit gains.

In the Midst of Silence

Whispers float through the air,
Echoes dance without a care.
The stillness wraps like a shawl,
In the hush, we hear it all.

Stars blink softly in the night,
Moonbeams cast a gentle light.
Thoughts wander, drifting away,
In silence, they long to play.

Heartbeat slows, a calm embrace,
Time dilutes in this quiet space.
Voices fade, dreams take their flight,
In the midst, we find our sight.

Moments linger, soft and sweet,
Gentle rhythms guide our beat.
In silence, we truly hear,
The beauty that draws us near.

A Lullaby in the Dark

Night descends with a sigh,
A lullaby to the sky.
Softly hush the waking world,
In dreams, our sails are unfurled.

Moonlit whispers gently sway,
Guiding hearts that yearn to stay.
Stars like lanterns softly gleam,
Cradling us in a tender dream.

Shadows dance with a soothing grace,
In dark corners, love finds its place.
Each and every night will sing,
A lullaby that hopes to bring.

Rest your head, let troubles cease,
In the dark, we find our peace.
So close your eyes and drift away,
To the melody of the day.

Reflections from the Void

In the depths where echoes fade,
A mirror shows the dreams we made.
Silent realms of thought and sighs,
Whisper truths that never die.

Shadows speak of what once was,
In the stillness, we pause because.
Fragments lost yet still remain,
In empty spaces, we find gain.

The void holds secrets deep within,
An endless journey where we begin.
Reflections dance, elusive and bright,
Guiding souls through the darkest night.

In silence lies a hidden art,
From the void, we make our start.
With every thought, every embrace,
We weave the fabric of our space.

The Void's Embrace

In the void, time seems to freeze,
A gentle touch, a soft, warm breeze.
Darkness wraps around like a quilt,
In its arms, all fears are stilled.

Here in absence, we find our way,
Navigating night, come what may.
The quiet calls with whispers clear,
In the void, all is sincere.

Stars above like distant friends,
In the void, our journey bends.
Each heartbeat echoes soft and low,
A symphony only we can know.

In the embrace of shadows deep,
A bond is formed in silence steep.
The void shows love in its purest form,
In emptiness, we are reborn.

The Cosmic Pulse of Isolation

In the silence of the night, we drift,
Stars whisper secrets, softly rift.
Galaxies spin, a dance unseen,
Alone in the cosmos, lost in between.

Echoes of time in the dark unfold,
Threads of existence, fragile and bold.
Every heartbeat a distant flare,
Waves of longing entwined in despair.

Light-years stretch in quiet disdain,
Bound by the stars, but trapped in the pain.
Gravity tugs at the soul's retreat,
Yet still we yearn for a heartbeat complete.

Isolation's pulse, a rhythm so bright,
Illuminates shadows, igniting the night.
In the vastness, we seek to connect,
In the cosmic glow, our fears to reject.

Soliloquies of the Heart's Hollow

Whispers echo in the empty space,
Words unspoken, time cannot erase.
The heart's hollow sings a weary tune,
A dance of shadows beneath a pale moon.

Thoughts swirl quietly, like autumn leaves,
In solitude, the heart quietly grieves.
Each sigh is a story held close inside,
In the silence, the echoes abide.

Cloaked in longing, the soul's tender plea,
A soliloquy wrapped in mystery.
Searching the depths for a flicker of light,
In the shadows, we find our plight.

Yet in this space, a flicker remains,
A spark of hope that breaks through the chains.
In the heart's hollow, an ember glows,
Promising warmth that gently bestows.

Reflections in a Shattered Mirror

Fragments shimmer, reality bends,
Faces blur, where the illusion ends.
In shards of glass, we seek the whole,
Reflections of a once united soul.

Each piece a story, a truth to reveal,
In the chaos, the heart learns to heal.
Dissonant echoes linger on the floor,
A symphony played through an open door.

Gathering remnants, we paint a new art,
From the brokenness, we make a start.
In the ruins, we find our way clear,
Learning to love what we once held dear.

Mirrored visions, a kaleidoscope view,
In the shattered, there lies something true.
Collecting the pieces, we craft our own fate,
In the reflections, we dare to create.

Cerulean Skies Behind Closed Eyes

Behind closed eyes, the world fades away,
A canvas of dreams where the heart can sway.
Cerulean skies stretch far and wide,
In the quiet, our spirit can glide.

Clouds of worry drift into the past,
In this sanctuary, we find peace at last.
Breath of freedom lifts the soul high,
Awakening wonders that shimmer and fly.

Colors of imagination spill from within,
Painting the horizons where dreams begin.
In this stillness, we gather our might,
A journey ignited by twinkling starlight.

So when the world outside feels too vast,
Take a moment, let the chaos be passed.
For behind closed eyes, the heart finds its way,
In cerulean whispers, we long to stay.

Embracing the Emptiness

In the stillness, shadows sigh,
Whispers lost in the silent sky.
Echoes fade like distant stars,
Holding space for what is ours.

Emptiness, a gentle friend,
A quiet heart where storms suspend.
Embracing voids of endless night,
Finding solace in the light.

Through the cracks, bright colors bleed,
In hollow places, hope's seed.
With every tear, we redefine,
The beauty found in the divine.

Letting go is learning how,
To bloom again from earth's soft brow.
In the void, we carve our place,
Embracing time with tender grace.

A Canvas of Invisible Colors

In the quiet, colors gleam,
Buried deep in a waking dream.
Brush strokes dance with unseen light,
Painting worlds beyond our sight.

Beyond the canvas, whispers play,
Invisible hues guide the way.
Each breath crafts art with silent flair,
A gallery of thoughts laid bare.

With every sigh, an unseen hue,
Mingling thoughts, both old and new.
Fragrant pastels, soft and true,
Life's palette shifts, and love breaks through.

In this space of vibrant grace,
We find ourselves, embrace our place.
A tapestry of silent sounds,
Where unseen beauty knows no bounds.

Gossamer Dreams on Velvet Air

Like whispers carried on the breeze,
Dreams drift softly through the trees.
Gossamer threads weave cosmic tales,
In the hush where magic trails.

Velvet air holds secrets tight,
Floating softly through the night.
Each dream a spark, a fleeting sigh,
A canvas painted in the sky.

With every heartbeat, wishes soar,
Gently nudging an open door.
In the stillness, hopes entwine,
Dancing lightly, sweet and divine.

On soft winds, we take our flight,
Floating free, hearts full and bright.
Gossamer dreams across the land,
In velvet air, we rise and stand.

Traces of Abandonment's Embrace

In quiet corners, memories fade,
Whispers linger where once they played.
Abandonment, a heavy shroud,
Yet softness rests within the crowd.

Dust settles on forgotten chairs,
Echoes haunt the empty squares.
Each trace speaks of stories lost,
A heavy heart bears all the cost.

Yet beauty blooms in barren lands,
From the ashes, life understands.
In every tear, a lesson stays,
A gentle reminder that hope stays.

In the silence, we find our way,
Through shadows cast by yesterday.
Embracing loss with tender grace,
Finding warmth in forgotten space.

A Tapestry of Solitary Nights

In shadows deep, my thoughts take flight,
Whispers weave through the still of night.
Stars above, like eyes that see,
Loneliness wraps its arms around me.

Each breath a thread, a silent song,
In the tapestry where I belong.
Moonlight dances on thoughts untold,
Crafting tales of the brave and bold.

Time stretches thin, a fragile line,
Embracing moments, feeling divine.
In solitude, I find my muse,
A canvas spun from dreams to choose.

The night unfolds, a velvet cloak,
As echoes of memory gently spoke.
In the hush, my heart ignites,
A tapestry of solitary nights.

Secrets Linger in Empty Spaces

In corners dim, where shadows play,
Secrets linger, hidden away.
Whispers soft, like a fragile thread,
Stories told where fears have bled.

Around each turn, silence reigns,
Echoes of laughter, forgotten chains.
In empty rooms, the past still breathes,
Woven tales in the dust that wreathes.

The floorboards creak with tales untold,
Echoes of warmth in a space grown cold.
Amongst the echoes, heartbeats sway,
Secrets linger, refusing to fray.

Each forgotten glance, a line on air,
In the stillness, they choose to share.
In empty spaces, memories chase,
Secrets linger, a sacred place.

Dreaming Beneath Celestial Silence

Under the vast and starry dome,
I find my heart, I find my home.
Dreams flutter softly, like fireflies,
In the silence, my spirit flies.

The midnight breeze, a gentle sigh,
Carries wishes as it sweeps by.
In tranquil moments, I seek the light,
Dreaming beneath the cloak of night.

A universe whispers in the dark,
Each star a lantern, each spark a mark.
Through endless skies, my thoughts cascade,
In celestial silence, fears do fade.

Floating on dreams, I drift away,
In the stillness, I choose to stay.
Beneath the stars, my soul takes flight,
Dreaming beneath celestial silence, bright.

The Art of Loneliness Unraveled

In quiet hours, I craft my bliss,
The art of loneliness, a fleeting kiss.
With every breath, I learn to soar,
In solitude, I unlock the door.

Colors swirl in a mind's embrace,
Each brushstroke speaks of time and space.
In isolation, I find my voice,
The art of loneliness, my chosen choice.

As canvases stretch before my eyes,
I paint my sorrows, my wildest cries.
Every shade whispers stories untold,
In the quiet, my heart grows bold.

The masterpiece, a world unseen,
Crafted in silence, serene and keen.
The art of loneliness, my secret reveal,
In every stroke, I learn to heal.

Unraveled Threads

Fraying edges of the mind,
Whispers lost in empty rooms.
Colors fade, once intertwined,
Time unwinds with silent glooms.

Tangled memories come alive,
In the shadows, truths collide.
Pieces scattered, yet they strive,
To find solace where they hide.

A tapestry of hopes and fears,
Sewn together, torn apart.
Through laughter, through the years,
Love still mends the fragile heart.

With every stitch, a tale unfolds,
Of dreams chased and lessons learned.
From the chaos, strength beholds,
In every thread, a spirit burned.

The Space Between Souls

In the quiet, whispers dwell,
A language only hearts can know.
Between the beats, a secret spell,
Where silence sings and shadows glow.

Moments shared, yet worlds apart,
Bound by feelings we can't see.
In the distance, a longing heart,
Echoes softly, 'Come to me.'

Stories woven in the night,
Two souls dance with gentle grace.
In the dark, they find their light,
In the space, they embrace space.

With every breath, a silent song,
A melody of dreams untold.
In this bond, where we belong,
Love persists, a thread of gold.

A Symphony of Solitude

In the stillness, music plays,
Notes that linger in the air.
A symphony of quiet days,
Where silence speaks, and hearts lay bare.

Each heartbeat resonates like drum,
A rhythm felt but seldom heard.
In solitude, we become
The quiet souls, their voices stirred.

Underneath a velvet sky,
Stars align in whispered tones.
Through the dark, we learn to fly,
In our own, familiar zones.

In the space of being alone,
Harmony finds its gentle way.
In solitude, strength has grown,
A symphony that will not sway.

Musing Beneath the Stars

Underneath this endless night,
Stars alight in cosmic dance.
Whispers float on dreams of light,
Infinite in every chance.

Thoughts take flight on gentle breeze,
Silent wishes ride the waves.
In this space, the heart finds ease,
In the darkness, soul behaves.

Galaxies, like scattered charms,
Invite us to explore the fate.
In their glow, there's warmth and arms,
Time slows down, we resonate.

Musing soft beneath the skies,
With each twinkle, visions play.
In the depths where wonder lies,
We find ourselves, we drift away.

The Labyrinth of Self

In corridors of thought, we wander,
Each turn a question, a silent ponder.
Reflections flicker, truth and lies,
In the maze of heart, each echo sighs.

Paths intertwine, with choices made,
Lost or found, in the cool cascade.
Whispers beckon, the search goes on,
The light of dawn breaks, hope is drawn.

Mirrors distort what we wish to see,
Yet fragments of love set the spirit free.
Through winding ways, we learn to dance,
In the labyrinth's heart, we're given a chance.

Each step we take, both bold and meek,
Leads to the essence of what we seek.
In the silence, we find our tone,
The labyrinth of self, we walk alone.

Shadows on the Wall

In the twilight's grasp, shadows play,
Whispered secrets of dusk and day.
Figures linger, stories unsaid,
On the canvas of night, they tread.

Flickering lights, a dance of dreams,
Haunting echoes in muted beams.
Footsteps follow, but none can trace,
The delicate waltz of time and space.

Every shadow holds a tale,
Of joy and sorrow, love's frail veil.
In the quiet, their voices blend,
A timeless journey that will not end.

Beneath the surface, we all conceal,
The hopes, the fears we refuse to feel.
On the wall, they sway and fall,
Eternal moments, shadows enthrall.

Waves of Respite

Gentle tides that kiss the shore,
Whispers of peace, forever more.
Each wave a sigh, a soft embrace,
Under the sky, we find our place.

Sands of time slip through our hands,
As we listen to the ocean's bands.
In every swell, a breath, a chance,
To find our rhythm, to dream, to dance.

Drifting thoughts like seagulls soar,
In the calm of night, our spirits roar.
The water's lull, a healing song,
In waves of respite, we all belong.

Let troubles fade with the ebbing tide,
In nature's arms, let our hearts abide.
For as the ocean's heart beats true,
We find our solace in its hue.

Solace in the Shadows

In the corners dim, where silence dwells,
Whispers of comfort in soft-spoken fells.
The night wraps tight, a cloak so warm,
In solace found, away from harm.

Each shadow drapes a gentle frame,
Of memories held, yet none the same.
In hidden depths, we start to see,
The beauty found in mystery.

Away from light, where fears may lurk,
In stillness, revealed, like an ancient work.
The dance of dusk brings healing grace,
In shadows deep, we find our place.

So let us wander, sidestep the glare,
For in the dim, there's much to share.
In every silhouette, a story calls,
Finding solace—our heart enthralls.

Serene in Solitude

In quiet corners where shadows play,
A tranquil heart finds its gentle way.
The whispers of wind through the trees,
Bring solace sweet like a warm breeze.

Soft moments linger, sweet and rare,
A solitude that lifts despair.
In nature's arms, I find my peace,
A silent world where troubles cease.

Glimmers of sunlight dance on leaves,
Each rustle knows what the heart believes.
In this embrace, I am alive,
Where dreams and quiet joys can thrive.

With every heartbeat, I feel its grace,
In solitude's arms, I find my place.
A sanctuary carved from the night,
Where silence holds both fear and light.

Scripting Absence

Words hang heavy, untouched by the pen,
Empty pages, a silence to comprehend.
Each line yearns for what once was near,
Echoes of laughter, now just a tear.

The ink runs dry in the absence you left,
A narrative lost, my heart feels bereft.
With each stroke, I trace your name,
In the margins of sorrow, nothing feels the same.

Memories linger like shadows at dusk,
Fleeting whispers, a fragile husk.
The stories we wove now frayed at the seams,
Scattered fragments of lost dreams.

Yet in this void, I find my release,
Creating worlds where pain can cease.
Scripting absence, a canvas anew,
Painting the silence with shades of you.

Lanterns Flicker in the Dark

In the stillness, lanterns glow bright,
Casting warmth on the edges of night.
Their flicker dances with shadows deep,
A guiding light where secrets keep.

With every breath, the darkness sighs,
Illuminating hopes, where courage lies.
Each lantern swings with stories untold,
Whispers of dreams, both timid and bold.

Beneath the stars, they twinkle and weave,
A tapestry of light for those who believe.
In these moments, we gather near,
Finding solace in glow, casting out fear.

Together we stand, hand in hand,
Beneath the lanterns, we take our stand.
Flickering flames that never depart,
A symbol of love, lighting the heart.

Shadows Where We Dwell

In corners dark, where shadows creep,
Echoes of laughter drift soft and deep.
Beneath the veil of twilight's reign,
Our secrets linger, a quiet refrain.

Fragmented light slips through the blinds,
A dance of whispers where hope unwinds.
In these shadows, our stories meet,
The pulse of the night, haunting and sweet.

As time unfolds, we intertwine,
In the fabric of silence, our hearts align.
Together we navigate the unseen,
In shadows where all that is, has been.

Through tangled dreams, we softly tread,
In the haunting glow where old paths led.
Finding comfort in the presence of friends,
As shadows embrace, the journey extends.

Whispers of a Forgotten Room

Dusty corners hold their breath,
Memories linger, soft as lace.
Faded whispers, tales of death,
In shadows dance, they find their place.

Sunlight streams through broken panes,
Casting ghosts on wooden floors.
Echoes of laughter, hint of pain,
A lonely heart that still explores.

Worn-out chairs and antique books,
Bear witness to the time long past.
In quiet nooks, the silence cooks,
A reverie that holds us fast.

Time moves slowly, like a sigh,
In this room where secrets bloom.
Letting go, yet asking why,
With every breath, we lift the gloom.

Threads of Quiet Reflection

In stillness deep, thoughts intertwine,
Moments captured, like a thread.
Each silent pause a chance to shine,
In gentle waves, the mind is led.

Beneath the weight of weary days,
A tapestry of dreams unfolds.
We weave our hopes in subtle ways,
Through whispers soft, our stories told.

Eyes closed tight against the light,
We journey through the unseen space.
Finding solace in the night,
In quietude, we find our grace.

With every stitch, a heart laid bare,
Threads of hope, of love, of fears.
In silence, wisdom fills the air,
We gather strength to meet the years.

The Dance of Distant Stars

In velvet skies, the stars align,
A cosmic waltz ignites the night.
Each twinkle is a whispered sign,
Of endless tales in fading light.

They spin and sway in silent grace,
Eternal partners in the dark.
Galaxies drift, their secret place,
With dreams that flicker, bright and stark.

Asteroids chase with playful gleam,
Comets trail with fiery tails.
In this vast space, we breathe a dream,
As stardust weaves its timeless trails.

With every glance, a wish ignites,
In the depths of night, we still dare.
To chase the glow of distant lights,
And find our selves among the rare.

Echoes in the Stillness

In a quiet room, echoes reside,
Soft as the breath of a whispered prayer.
Time slows down, in stillness we hide,
Finding solace in the muted air.

Each sound a ghost from days gone by,
Flickering memories softly play.
As silence deepens, we learn to fly,
On wings of sounds that drift away.

The clock ticks slow, a heartbeat's song,
Notes of longing threaded through space.
In echoes, we hear where we belong,
Lost in the beauty of time and grace.

A gentle pull, the pull of the heart,
In stillness, we connect the dots.
Where echoes dance and never part,
In the silence, we embrace our thoughts.

Echoes of Empty Rooms

In corners where silence clings,
Whispers of memories softly sing.
Faded light through cracked old glass,
Time stands still as moments pass.

Cobwebs dance in gentle breeze,
Old furniture bows with unease.
Each creak of wood, a weary sigh,
Where laughter lingered, now they lie.

Windows gaze upon the street,
Where once there was life, now defeat.
Echoes linger, shadows play,
In empty rooms, dreams drift away.

Yet hope remains in quiet grace,
As sun breaks through to touch this space.
A promise born in muted gloom,
Resides within these empty rooms.

When Shadows Speak

Beneath the glow of waning light,
Shadows stretch, prepare for flight.
They whisper secrets of the night,
In quiet corners, they ignite.

Darkness weaves its tapestry,
Of fears and hopes, a mystery.
In whispered tones, they share their tales,
As curving paths and moonlight trails.

Figures dance against the wall,
From flickering flames, their shadows fall.
Each moment breathed, a silent plea,
For echoes of what used to be.

So heed the whispers in the dark,
For shadows speak, they leave a mark.
In tender hush, their voice does swell,
To tell the stories we dare not tell.

The Language of Dust

In sunlight's beam, dust motes play,
Whirls of time in gentle sway.
Each grain a story left behind,
In corners where the past unwinds.

On forgotten shelves, layers stack,
Whispers of ages, never lack.
Binders of lives, in layers thick,
A silent language, soft and quick.

Touched by fingers, memories rise,
In clouds of dust, the heart replies.
Each sigh of air, a tale retold,
Of love and loss, of dreams grown cold.

So let us cherish, every speck,
For in the dust, we find respect.
The language spoken, through the years,
Is written clear, for those who hear.

Lanterns of Reflection

In twilight's glow, the lanterns gleam,
Casting shadows, a soft dream.
With every flicker, stories share,
Of paths once walked, of love and care.

Beneath their light, the past awakes,
In every flicker, a memory shakes.
Guiding lost souls; a gentle hand,
Through twisted roads, across the land.

As candles burn, the moments twine,
Reflections intertwine, divine.
In quiet circles, voices hum,
In lantern light, we all become.

So raise a glass to fleeting light,
To lanterns bright that pierce the night.
For in their glow, we find our way,
Through shadows deep, to greet the day.